Written by Noah Leatherland

SOCCER

PowerKiDS
press

Published in 2025
by The Rosen Publishing Group, Inc.
2544 Clinton Street, Buffalo, NY 14224

© 2024 BookLife Publishing Ltd.

Written by: Noah Leatherland
Edited by: E.C. Andrews
Designed by: Jasmine Pointer

Cataloging-in-Publication Data

Names: Leatherland, Noah, 1999-.
Title: Soccer / Noah Leatherland.
Description: Buffalo, NY : PowerKids Press, 2025. | Series: World of sports | Includes glossary and index.
Identifiers: ISBN 9781499449013 (pbk.) | ISBN 9781499449020 (library bound) | ISBN 9781499449037 (ebook)
Subjects: LCSH: Soccer--Juvenile literature.
Classification: LCC GV943.25 L384 2025 | DDC 796.334--dc23

Manufactured in the United States of America
CPSIA Compliance Information: Batch #CW25PK. For further information contact Rosen Publishing at 1-800-237-9932.

Find us on 

IMAGE CREDITS

All images are courtesy of Shutterstock.com. With thanks to Getty Images, Thinkstock Photo and iStockphoto.
Cover – Master1305, Akito Studio, Alice July, je48design. Throughout – je48design. 4–5 – matimix, Fotokostic. 6–7 – Bukharev Oleg, anek.soowannaphoom. 8–9 – mooinblack, enterlinedesign, Jose Breton- Pics Action. 10–11 – MaciejGillert, IOIO IMAGES. 12–13 – Thx4Stock team, Gorodenkoff. 14–15 – U. J. Alexander, Dziurek, Review News. 16–17 – Victor Velter, ph.FAB. 18–19 – Ollyy, Tusumaru, matimix, katatonia82. 20–21 – A.RICARDO, Mikolaj Barbanell. 22–23 – Drazen Zigic, PeopleImages. com - Yuri A.

CONTENTS

WORDS THAT LOOK LIKE THIS CAN BE FOUND IN THE GLOSSARY ON PAGE 24.

Sports are something that anyone can take part in. Sports push you to try your best and work with others as a team. What sports do you like to play?

Soccer is the most <u>popular</u> sport in the world. Millions of people play soccer, watch games on TV, and have a favorite team that they support. Soccer is all about teamwork.

THE BASICS

A game of soccer is played by two teams of eleven players. Each team has a few <u>substitute</u> players who can swap in for someone on the field. Games are 90 minutes long.

The aim of a game of soccer is to score more points than the other team. A point is scored when the ball is put into the **opponent's** goal.

7

POSITIONS

Goalkeeper

Each team has one goalkeeper. Their job is to stop the other team from scoring. Goalkeepers are allowed to use their hands to block shots and pick up the ball.

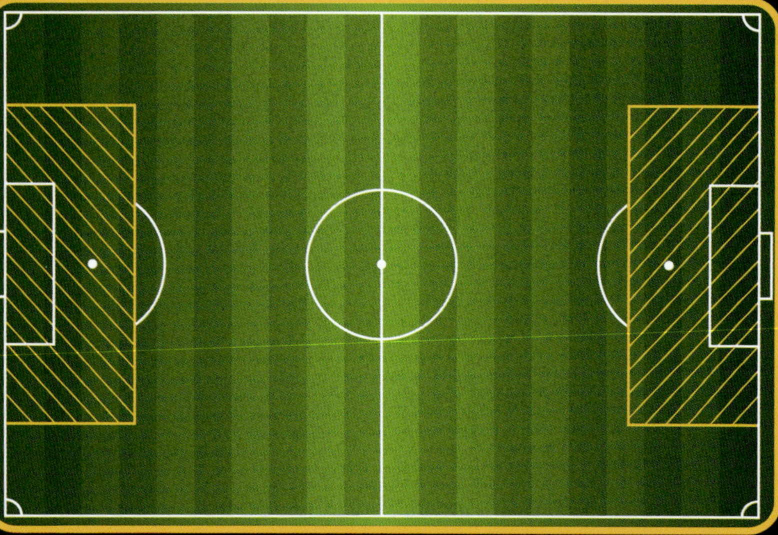

Goalkeepers can only use their hands inside the box marked around their goal.

A defender's job is to stop the other team from getting close to their goal. Defenders have to be good at tackling. Tackling is when a player gets the ball away from an opponent.

Midfielder

A midfielder plays in the middle part of the pitch. They help their team defend and attack. Midfielders have to be good at passing so that their team can move the ball forward.

Forward

A forward plays closer to the opponent's goal. Their job is to score goals for their team. Forwards have to be good at shooting the ball. Shooting means kicking the ball towards the goal.

TACTICS

Soccer teams go into games with a set of <u>tactics</u>. Teams can set up in whatever <u>formation</u> they like. Some teams play with more forwards. Others play with more defenders.

Different teams like to play with different styles. Some teams like to play with fast, short passes. Others like to use long passes to get past opponents. There are lots of ways to play.

FOULS

A foul is **committed** when a player does something against the rules. Fouls include hurting another player when making a tackle and outfield players touching the ball with their hands.

Referees can warn players who are committing fouls by giving them a yellow card. If a player commits a really bad foul, the referee can give them a red card and send them off the pitch.

If a player gets two yellow cards, they are given a red card.

Gameplay stops when a foul is committed. The game is started again by a free kick made by the team that was fouled. Free kicks can be good chances to score goals.

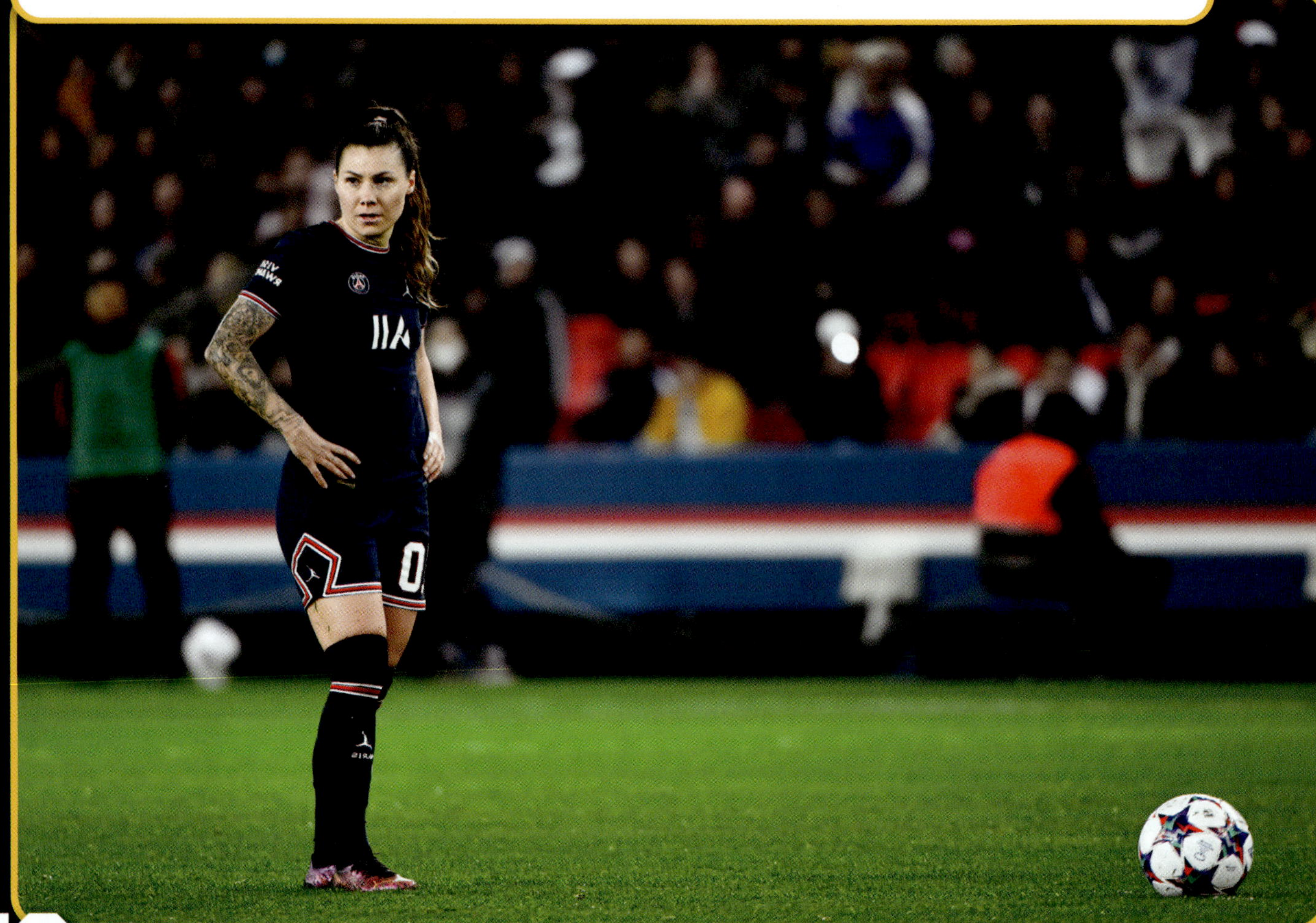

If a player commits a foul inside their goalkeeper's box, the other team is given a penalty kick. This is a shot taken from the spot marked on the ground.

OUT-OF-BOUNDS

Pitch markings

Knocking the ball over the edge of the pitch gives the other team **possession** of the ball.

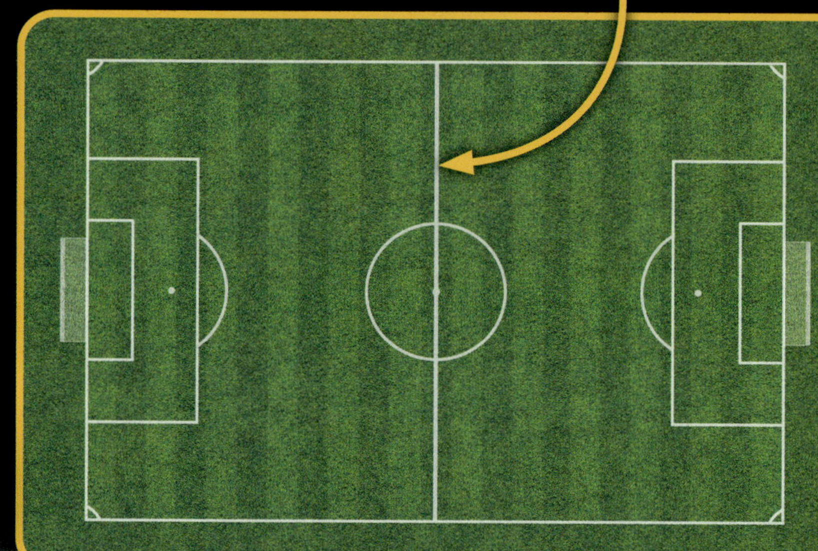

Throw-Ins

If the ball goes over the long edge of the pitch, it is thrown back in.

Goal Kicks

Goalkeepers are given goal kicks when their opponents knock the ball out near their goal.

Corner Kicks

Teams get a corner kick if their opponents knock the ball out near their own goal.

THE WORLD CUP

The World Cup is the biggest soccer competition in the world. It is held every four years. Every country in the world has a chance to take part in the competition.

World Cup matches are played in huge stadiums in front of thousands of fans. For many soccer players, playing for their country in the World Cup is a dream come true.

WORLD OF SPORTS

People play and watch soccer all over the world. There are hundreds of different clubs, big and small. Is there a team you support? Would you like to play for them one day?

Is soccer a game that you already play, or would you like to start? You could play with your friends or see if there is a team you could join!

GLOSSARY

commit	carry out an action
formation	where a team puts its players on the pitch
opponent	someone on the team one is playing against. Also, the team one is playing against.
popular	liked by many people
possession	when one team has control of the ball
style	way that something is done
substitute	something that replaces something else
tactics	planned ways of doing something

INDEX